The experiential learning theory of career development

David A. Kolb, Mark S. Plovnick

Nabu Public Domain Reprints:

You are holding a reproduction of an original work published before 1923 that is in the public domain in the United States of America, and possibly other countries. You may freely copy and distribute this work as no entity (individual or corporate) has a copyright on the body of the work. This book may contain prior copyright references, and library stamps (as most of these works were scanned from library copies). These have been scanned and retained as part of the historical artifact.

This book may have occasional imperfections such as missing or blurred pages, poor pictures, errant marks, etc. that were either part of the original artifact, or were introduced by the scanning process. We believe this work is culturally important, and despite the imperfections, have elected to bring it back into print as part of our continuing commitment to the preservation of printed works worldwide. We appreciate your understanding of the imperfections in the preservation process, and hope you enjoy this valuable book.

WORKING PAPER
ALFRED P. SLOAN SCHOOL OF MANAGEMENT

The Experiential Learning Theory
of Career Development

David A. Kolb
Mark S. Plovnick

M.I.T. Working Paper #705-74   May, 1974

MASSACHUSETTS
INSTITUTE OF TECHNOLOGY
50 MEMORIAL DRIVE
CAMBRIDGE, MASSACHUSETTS 02139

The Experiential Learning Theory
of Career Development

David A. Kolb
Mark S. Plovnick

M.I.T. Working Paper #705-74   May, 1974

Paper prepared for the MIT/ILP Conference on Career Development, 22 May 1974
Not to be reproduced or quoted without permission of the authors

HJ28
M414
no.705-74

While much is known in increasing detail about the processes and stages of development in children and adolescents, there has been comparitively little research on the developmental regularities in the lives of adult men and women. This scarcity of empirically based scientific models of development is paralleled by the primitive nature of popular common sense images of adult life, e.g. "they were married and lived happily ever after" and the notion of a "success ladder" to be climbed rung after rung.

One major reason for the failure to formulate more articulate models of adult development has to do with the difficulty of conceptualizing adult development. While the worlds of children and even adolescents are structurely similar, the worlds of adults becomes highly differentiated along a great number of dimensions. This problem of complexity has led to either generalized self-environment process models of career development (e.g. Super et al. 1963) or deterministic models of personality development that trace different career paths to formative experiences in those well known early years of development (e.g. Roe, 1956; McClelland, 1962) or to linear one track models of adult development that describe a normative path for human growth that is precipitated through periodic crises of environmental adaptation (e.g. Erickson, 1959, Levinson, unpublished M.S. thesis) or to the familiar trait-factor approach to career development that focuses on some one or more personal variables as the determinants of career choice which is seen as only one decision, i.e. the first job choice (e.g. Holland, 1973). While it is not out task here to examine and critique these different approaches in detail, suffice it to say the approach of this discussion is to integrate what we feel to be the strengths of each of the above theoretical strategies. More specifically we are attempting in the formulation of the experiential learning theory of adult development to create an approach that (1) gives a central role to self-environment interaction, (2) describes differentiated paths of adult development, (3) maintains an emphasis on a normative model of human fulfillment, and (4) focuses on certain specific personal variables that can be used to understand and influence the career development process.

Stability and Change in Career Development

Any comprehensive theory of career development must explain not only the emergence of stable enduring career paths, but it must also explain the dynamics and directions of career change. In the experiential learning theory of adult development stability and change in career paths is seen as resulting from the interaction between internal personality dynamics and external social forces in a manner much like that described by Super (Super et.al 1963). The most

powerful developmental dynamic that emerges from this interaction is the tendency for there to be a closer and closer match between self characteristics and environmental demands. This match comes about in two ways -- 1) environments tend to change personal characteristics to fit them, i.e socialization and, 2) individuals tend to select themselves into environments that are consistent with their personal characteristics Thus career development in general tends to follow a path toward accentuation of personal characteristics and skills (Feldman & Newcomb 1969, Kolb, 1973b) in that development is a product of the interaction between choices and socialization experiences that match these dispositions and the resulting experiences further reinforce the same choice disposition for later experience. Many adult life paths follow a cycle of job, educational and life style choices that build upon the experiences resulting from previous similar choices. Indeed the common sterotype of the successful career is a graded ladder of similar experiences on which one climbs to success and fulfillment.

Yet accentuation represents only the warp of the fabric of adult career development. The woof is formed by the career changes that mark transitions from one career path to another

Given this primary developmental force toward stable, linear career paths, we suggest that change or deviation from this career path can occur in only three ways

1 The individual may err in his choice of a matching socialization experience. For example, the woman with scientific interest may not choose a scientific career on the "good advice" that there are few jobs for women in science. Or an individual may decide to become an engineer because he has been told how glamourous it is, even though he at present doesn't like mathematics or science very much

2. The socialization experience may cease to reward the choice dispositions and skills that brought the individual to it This is the career cul de sac where the individual is rewarded for accentuation of his personal skills and dispositions up to a given point where further advancement or development is precluded unless he or she is prepared to develop new knowledge, skills or attitudes For example, engineers in most organizations reach a point where further advancement or promotion is possible only by moving into management Studies of engineers and managers (e g. Sofer, 1970, Jaffe, 1971) indicate

that lack of success and advancement are major factors in mid-career crises. The women in the housewife or mother role experiences this change in another way. A husband's increasing success and development can cause her role as a wife to change dramatically, leaving homemaking satisfactions abandoned. Similarly as children grow up and leave home the nurturent mother role becomes irrelevant. Gail Sheehy (1974) describes well how complex these dynamics can be

> "Now invigorated by his new-found confidence, no longer in constant need of having his loneliness "taken care of" and having become bored by a substitute mother, he changes the instructions to his wife, now you must be something more too. Be a companion instead of a child or mother, be capable of excellence like me. "Why don't you take some courses" is the way it usually comes out, because he doesn't want her to stray too far from the caretaking of him (and children if they have or plan them). But what he sees as "encounaging" her, she perceives as threatening her, getting rid of her, freeing himself from her, because this relationship has become mutually restricting
>
> She is at war with her own age 30 inner demons, but ill equipped to be "something more." As part of their earlier collusion, she was told she didn't have to get out in the world in any full sense. She could become her mother in her own married household. So long as she does not individuate, she can partake in all those illusions which she brought along from her own mother that make her feel safe. Anyone who pushes the other way is goading her toward danger." (pg 34-35)

3. <u>The individual as a result of his own maturation and personality development may find that his personal style and choice dispositions change, placing these new desires in conflict with the accentuating socialization process he has chosen.</u> For example, there is a general tendency for undergraduate students to move away from interests in science to the social sciences, arts and humanities (Davis, 1965) Our own research (Plovnick, 1971, 1972, Kolb, 1973b) and counseling with students at MIT has illustrated how difficult and traumatic this conflict can be. A sophomore engineering student who has suddenly discovered the excitement of psychology and human behavior must now face the difficult decision of transfering to another school or making do with the resources at hand. The corresponding conflict can occur for the practicing engineer whose years of impersonal isolation in the world of things becomes boring and he finds new interest in personal relationships with family and fiiends, and co-workers

Experiential Learning Theory and Adult Development

From the psychological perspective the developmental cycle of choices and experiences is seen as a process of learning. Experiential learning theory provides a means of conceptualizing the learning process that allows for the identification of different learning styles and corresponding environments that are congruent with these learning styles. Thus the theory offers a framework for mapping career paths that follow the accentuation pattern (i.e. toward a greater match between learning style and its corresponding environment) and those paths that deviate from this pattern. The learning model is a dialectic one, founded on the Jungian (Jung, 1923) concept of styles or types that states that fulfillment in adult development is accomplished by higher level integration and expression of non-dominant modes of dealing with the world. This concept of fulfillment forms the basis for predictions about the directions of career transition.

The theory is called "experiential learning" for two reasons. The first is historical, tieing it to its intellectual origins in the social psychology of Kurt Lewin in the 40's and the sensitivity training and laboratory education work of the 50's and 60's. The second reason is to emphasize the important role that experience plays in the learning process, an emphasis that differentiates this approach from other cognitive theories of the learning process. The core of the model is a simple description of the learning cycle, of how experience is translated into concepts which in turn are used as guides in the choice of new experiences.

Figure 1
The Experiential Learning Model

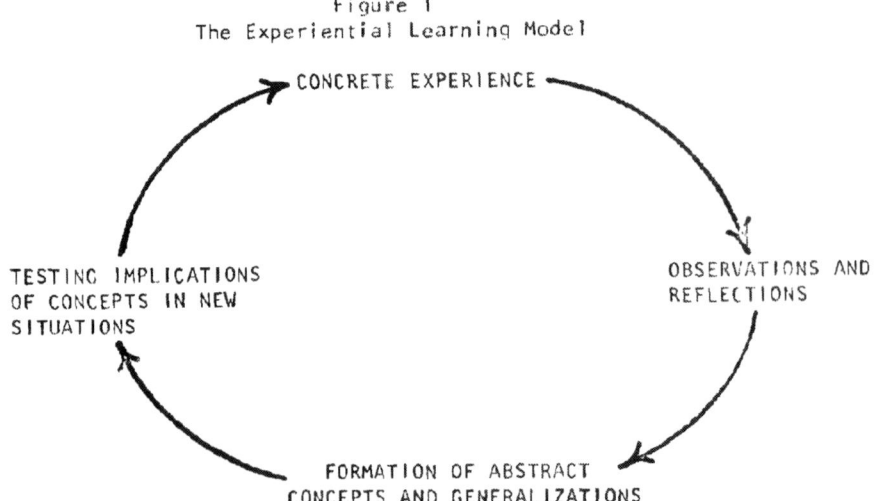

Learning is conceived as a four stage cycle. Immediate concrete experience is the basis for observation and reflection. These observations are assimilated into a "theory" from which new implications for action can be deduced. These implications or hypotheses then serve as guides in acting to create new experiences. The learner, if he is to be effective, needs four different kinds of abilities -- <u>Concrete Experience</u> abilities (CE), <u>Reflective Observation</u> abilties (RO), <u>Abstract Conceptualization</u> abilities (AC) and <u>Active Experimentation</u> (AE) abilities That is, he must be able to involve himself fully, openly, and without bias in new experiences (CE), he must be able to reflect on and observe these experiences from many perspectives (RO); he must be able to create concepts that integrate his observations into logically sound theories (AC) and he must be able to use these theories to make decisions and solve problems (AE). Yet this ideal is difficult to achieve. Can anyone become highly skilled in all of these abilities or are they necessarily in conflict? How can one act and reflect at the same time? How can one be concrete and immediate and still be theoretical?

A closer examination of the four-stage learning model would suggest that learning requires abilities that are polar opposites and that the learner, as a result, must continually choose which set of learning abilities he will bring to bear in any specific learning situation. More specifically, there are two primary dimensions to the learning process. The first dimension represents the concrete experiencing of events at one end and abstract conceptualization at the other. The other dimension has active experimentation at one extreme and reflective observation at the other. Thus, in the process of learning one moves in varying degrees from actor to observer, from specific involvement to general analytic detachment

Many cognitive psychologists (e g Flavell, 1963, Bruner, 1960, 1966, Harvey, Hunt & Shroeder, 1961) have identified the concrete/abstract dimension as a primary dimension on which cognitive growth and learning occurs Goldstein and Scheerer suggest that greater abstractness results in the development of the following abilities:

1. To detach our ego from the outer world or from inner experience
2. To assume a mental set
3. To account for acts to oneself, to verbalize the account
4. To shift reflectively from one aspect of the situation to another
5. To hold in mind simultaneously various aspects
6. To grasp the essential of a given whole; to break up a given into parts to isolate and to synthesize them
7. To abstract common properties reflectively; to form hierarchic concepts
8. To plan ahead ideationally, to assume an attitude toward the more possible and to think or perform symbolically (1941, p 4)

Concreteness, on the other hand, represents the absence of these abilities, the immersion in and domination by one's immediate experiences. Yet as the circular, dialectic model of the learning process would imply, abstractness is not exclusively good and concreteness exclusively bad. To be creative requires that one be able to experience anew, freed somewhat from the constraints of previous abstract concepts In psychoanalytic theory this need for a concrete childlike perspective in the creative process is referred to as regression in service of the ego (Kris, 1952). Bruner (1966) in his essay on the conditions for creativity further emphasizes the dialectic tension between abstract and concrete involvement. For him the creative act is a product of detachment and commitment, of passion and decorum, and of a freedom to be dominated by the object of one's inquiry.

The active/reflective dimension is the other major dimension of cognitive growth and learning As growth occurs, thought becomes more reflective and internalized, based more on the manipulation of symbols and images than overt

actions. The modes of active experimentation and reflection, like abstractness/concreteness, stand in opposition to one another. Reflection tends to inhibit action and visa-versa. For example, Singer (1968) has found that children who have active internal fantasy lives are more capable of inhibiting action for long periods of time than are children with little internal fantasy life. Kagan, et al (1964) have found, on the other hand, that very active orientations toward learning situations inhibit reflection and thereby preclude the development of analytic concepts. Herein lies the second major dialectic in the learning process -- the tension between actively testing the implications of one's hypotheses and reflectively interpreting data already collected.

Individual Learning Styles and the Learning Style Inventory

Overtime, accentuation forces operate on individuals in such a way that the dialectic tensions between these dimensions are consistently resolved in a characteristic fashion. As a result of our hereditary equipment, our particular past life experience, and the demands of our present environment most people develop learning styles that emphasize some learning abilities over others. Through socialization experiences in family, school and work we come to resolve the conflicts between being active and reflective and between being immediate and analytical in characteristic ways. Some people develop minds that excell at assimilating disparate facts into coherent theories, yet these same people are incapable of, or uninterested in deducing hypotheses from their theory. Others are logical geniuses but find it impossible to involve and surrender themselves to an experience. And so on. A mathematician may come to place great emphasis on abstract concepts while a poet may value concete experience more highly. A manager may be primarily concerned with the active application of ideas while a naturalist may develop his observational skills highly. Each of us in a unique way develops a learning style that has some weak and strong points. We have developed a simple self-description inventory, the Learning Style Inventory (LSI), that is designed to measure an individual's strengths and weaknesses as a learner. The LSI measures an individual's relative emphasis on the four learning abilities -- Concrete Experience (CE), Reflective Observation (RO), Abstract Conceptualization (AC) and Active Experimentation (AE) by asking him, several different times, to rank order four words that describe these different abilities. For example, one set of four words is "Feeling" (CE), "Watching" (RO), "Thinking" (AC), "Doing" (AE). The inventory yields six scores, CE, RO, AC, and AE plus two

combination scores that indicate the extent to which an individual emphasizes abstractness over concreteness (AC-CE) and the extent to which an individual emphasizes active experimentation over reflection (AE-RO)

The LSI was administered to 800 practicing managers and graduate students in management to obtain norms for the management population. In general these managers tended to emphasize Active Experimentation over Reflective Observation. In addition, managers with graduate degrees tended to rate their abstract (AC) learning skills higher.[1] While the individuals we tested showed many different patterns of scores on the LSI, we have identified four statistically prevalent types of learning styles. We have called these four styles -- the Converger, the Diverger, the Assimilator, and the Accommodator.[2] The following is a summary of the characteristics of these types based both on our research and clinical observation of these patterns of LSI scores.

The <u>Converger's</u> dominant learning abilities are Abstract Conceptualization (AC) and Active Experimentation (AE). His greatest strength lies in the practical application of ideas. We have called this learning style the "Converger" because a person with this style seems to do best in those situations like conventional intelligence tests where there is a single correct answer or solution to a question or problem (<u>cf</u> Torrealba, 1972). His knowledge is organized in such a way that, through hypothetical-deductive reasoning, he can focus it on specific problems. Liam Hudson's (1966) research in this style of learning (using different measures than the LSI) shows that convergers are relatively unemotional, preferring to deal with things rather than people. They tend to have narrow interests, and choose to specialize in the physical sciences. Our research shows that this learning style is characteristic of many engineers (Kolb, 1973).

The <u>Diverger</u> has the opposite learning strengths of the convergers. He is best at Concrete Experience (CE) and Reflective Observation (RO). His greatest strength lies in his imaginative ability. He excells in the ability to view concrete situations from many perspectives and to organize many relationships into a meaningful "gestalt". We have labelled this style "Diverger" because a person with this type performs better in situations that call for generation of ideas such as a "brainstorming" idea session. Hudson's (1966) work on this particular learning style shows that divergers are interested in people and tend to be imaginative and emotional. They have broad cultural interests and tend to specialize in the arts. Our research show that this style is characteristic of persons with humanities and liberal arts backgrounds.

The <u>Assimilator's</u> dominant learning abilities are Abstract Conceptualization (AC) and Reflective Observation (RO). His greatest strength lies in his ability to create theoretical models. He excells in inductive reasoning, in assimilating disparate observations into an integrated explanation (Growchow, 1973). He, like the converger, is less interested in people and more concerned with the practical use of theories. For him it is more important that the theory be logically sound and precise. As a result, this learning style is more characteristic of the basic sciences and mathematics rather than the applied sciences. In oragnizations this learning style is found most often in the research and planning departments (Kolb, 1973; Strasmore, 1973).

The <u>Accommodator</u> has the opposite strengths of the Assimilator. He is best at Concrete Experience (CE) and Active Experimentation (AE). His greatest strength lies in doing things, in carrying out plans and experiments and involving himself in new experiences. He tends to be more of a risk-taker than people with the other three learning styles. We have labelled this style "Accommodator" because he tends to excel in those situations where he must adapt himself to specific immediate circumstances. He tends to solve problems in an intuitive trial and error manner (Growchow, 1973) relying heavily on other people for information rather than his own analytic ability (Stabell, 1973).

Learning Styles and Career Paths

If we examine the undergraduate majors of the individuals in our sample a correspondence can be seen between their LSI scores and their initial career interests. This is done by plotting the average LSI scores for managers in our sample who reported their undergraduate college major (only those majors with more than 10 people responding are included). The distribution of undergraduate majors on the learning style grid is quite consistent with theory.[3] Undergraduate business majors tend to have accommodative learning styles while engineers on the average fall in the convergent quadrent. History, English, political science and psychology majors all have divergent learning styles. Mathematics and chemistry majors have assimilative learning styles along with economics and sociology. Physics majors are very abstract falling between the convergent and assimilative quadrent. What these data show is that one's undergraduate education is a major factor in the development of his learning style. Whether this is because individual's are shaped by the fields they enter or because of the selection processes that put people into and out of disciplines is an open question at this point. Most probably both factors are operating -- people choose fields which are consistent with their learning styles and are further shaped to fit the learning norms of their field

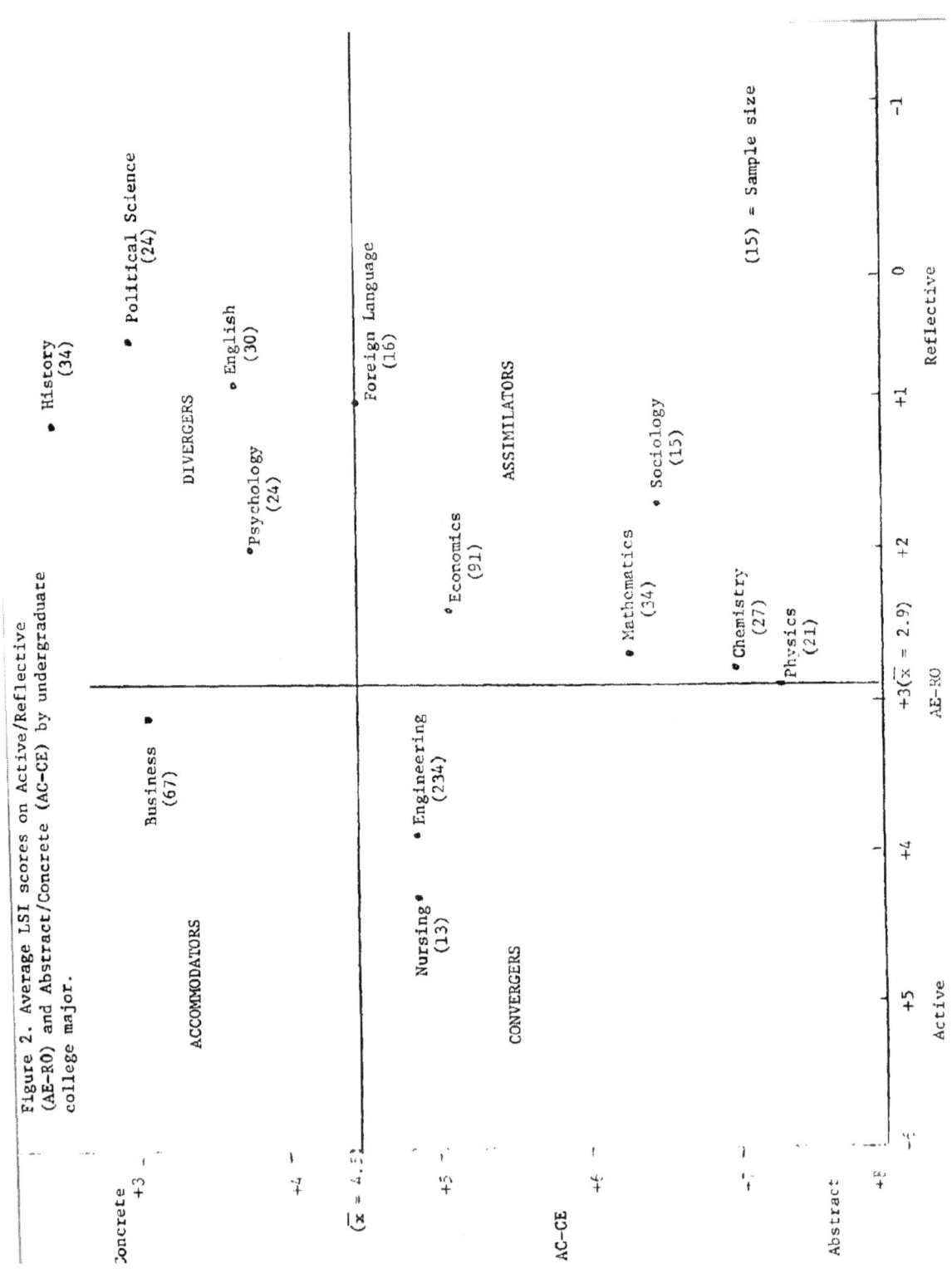

Figure 2. Average LSI scores on Active/Reflective (AE-RO) and Abstract/Concrete (AC-CE) by undergraduate college major.

once they are in it. When there is a mismatch between the fields learning norm's and the individuals learning style people will either change or leave the field

To examine if there was a correspondence between learning styles and the kind of jobs individuals held in mid-career we studies about 20 managers from each of five functional groups in a midwestern division of a large American industrial corporation. The five functional groups are described below followed by our hypothesis about the learning style that should characterize each group given the nature of their work

1. Marketing (n=20). This group is made up primarily of former salesmen. They have a non-quantitative "intuitive" approach to their work Because of their practical sales orientation in meeting customer demand they should have accommodative learning styles, i e concrete and active

2. Research (n=22). The work of this group is split about 50/50 between pioneer research and applied research projects. The emphasis is on basic research. Researchers should be the most assimilative group, i e , abstract and reflective, a style fitted to the world of knowledge and ideas

3. Personnel/Labor Relations (n=20) In this company men from this department serve two primary functions, interpreting personnel policy and promoting interaction among groups to reduce conflict and disagreement Because of their "people orientation" these men should be predominantly divergers, concrete and reflective

4. Engineering (n=18). This group is made up primarily of design engineers who are quite production oriented. They should be the most convergent subgroup, i.e., abstract and active, although they should be less abstract than the research group. They represent a bridge between thought and action.

5. Finance (n=20). This group has a strong computer, information systems bias. Finance men given their orientation toward the mathematical task of information system design should be highly abstract. Their crucial role in organizational survival should produce an active orientation. Thus finance group members should have convergent learning styles

Figure 3 shows the average scores on the active/reflective (AE-RO) and abstract/concrete (AC-CE) learning dimensions for the five functional groups. These results are consistent with the above predictions with the exception of the finance group whose scores are less active than predicted and thus they fall between the assimilative and the convergent quadrant.[4] The LSI clearly differentiates the learning styles that characterize managers following different career paths within a single company.

Evidence for Accentuation in Early Career

While the above data are suggestive of some general correspondence between learning styles and careers they do not offer direct evidence for the accentuation process. In a first attempt to examine the details of this process Plovnick (1971) studied a major university department using the concepts of convergence and divergence defined by Hudson (1966). He concluded that the major emphasis in physics education was on convergent learning. He predicted that physics students who had convergent learning styles would be content with their majors whereas physics majors who were divergent in their learning styles would be more uncertain of physics as a career and would take more courses outside of the physics department than their convergent colleagues. His predictions were confirmed. Those students who were not fitted for the convergent learning style required in physics tended to turn away from physics as a profession.

In another study currently in progress Plovnick (1974) is attempting to identify a correspondence between the learning style of medical students and their choices for career specialization. In addition he is attempting to identify relationships between learning styles and the process these students go through in making these choices. Initial data indicate that the different medical career

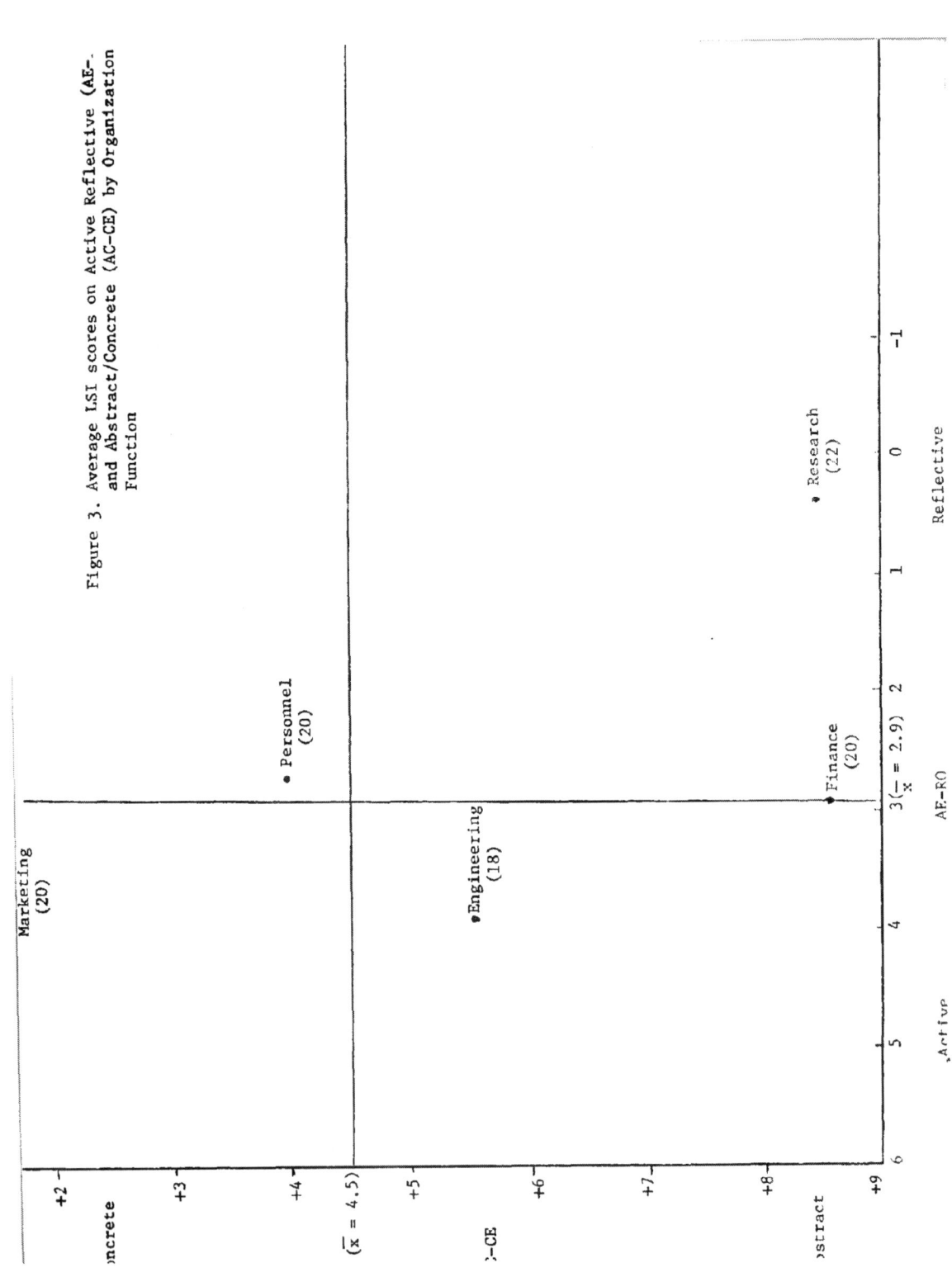

Figure 3. Average LSI scores on Active Reflective (AE-RO) and Abstract/Concrete (AC-CE) by Organization Function

paths (e.g. academic medicine, private practice, public health, etc.) attract people with different characteristic learning styles. Those that have styles that do not "match" their chosen career path indicate great uncertainty about whether they will continue to pursue that path. Further, students with different styles seem to be utilizing different sources of information and influence in the career development process. For example, concrete students seem to do more "identification" with attractive role models while abstract-reflective students are influenced more by course work. These "choices" about sources of influence then act to accentuate the learning style that led to the choice, since courses are inclined to more more abstract/reflective while close personal relationships are inclined to reinforce a more concrete style

In an unpublished study we examined the accentuation process as it operated at the molecular level of course choice. This research examined the choice of sensitivity training by MIT graduate students in management. When we tested the learning styles of students who chose an elective sensitivity training laboratory, we found that they tended to be more concrete (CE) and reflective (RO) than those who chose not to attend the lab. When these individuals with divergent learning styles completed the training sessions their scores became even more concrete and reflective, accentuating their disposition toward divergent learning experiences.

In a large survey of MIT seniors (Kolb, 1973b) we examined the correspondence between the learning styles of these students and their departmental majors and then compared these scores with the scores of those students who were continuing graduate study in their chosen major. The results of these analysis are shown graphically in Figure 4 for departments with 10 or more students. Analysis of variance for the six learning style dimensions by departmental majors shows that Reflective Observation, Active Experimentation, and the combination score active-reflective all vary significantly by departmental major. Differences on the abstract-concrete dimensions show no significance. This lack of significant differentiation may well be because of more uniform selective and normative pressures toward abstraction that operate across all the MIT departments

The correspondence between learning style and undergraduate major in this study are similar to the previous findings. Humanities falls in the diverger quadrent while mathematics is assimilative. Management is clearly accommodative. Although the engineering departments all fall on the lower edge of the accommodator quadrent rather than the converger quadrent as we would predict, this is most likely a function of the general abstract bias of MIT just noted. Physics and chemistry are not as abstract and reflective as predicted, although if the LSI scores of only those students planning to attend graduate school are used (as indicated by the

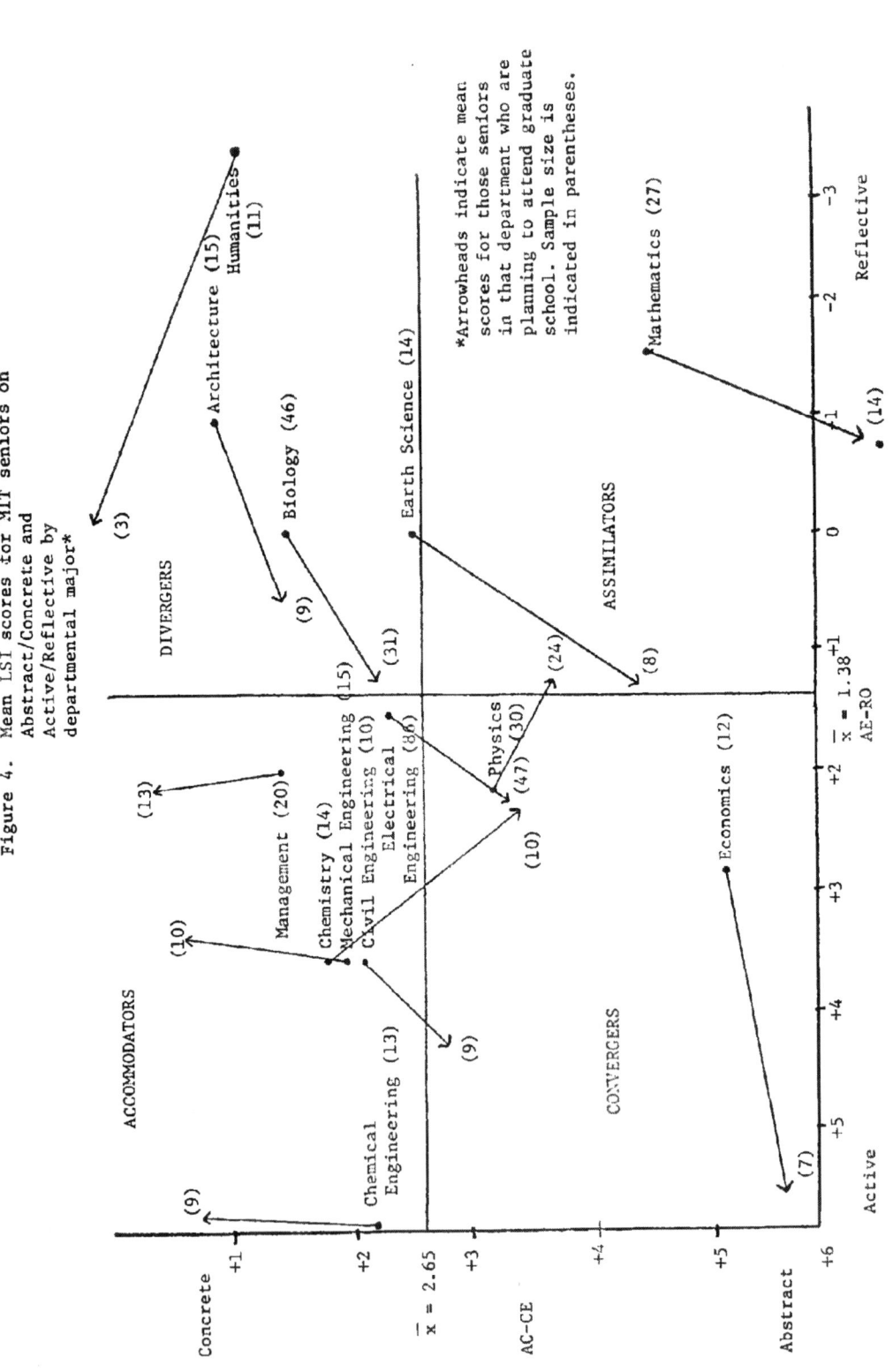

Figure 4. Mean LSI scores for MIT seniors on Abstract/Concrete and Active/Reflective by departmental major*

*Arrowheads indicate mean scores for those seniors in that department who are planning to attend graduate school. Sample size is indicated in parentheses.

arrowheads in Figure 4) the pattern is more consistent with prediction. Economics is somewhat more abstract and active than in our previous sample though this is somewhat a function of the unique nature of the MIT department. The architecture department's position in the divergent quadrent is also to some extent a function of the unique nature of the department with its emphasis on creative design and photography as well as the more convergent technical skills of architecture. We did not make predictions about the biology and earth science departments.

Figure 4 also contains data about career paths of the students in each of the departments. The arrowheads indicate for each department the average LSI scores for those students who are planning to attend graduate school. Our prediction was that those who chose to pursue a given discipline further through graduate training should show accentuation of the learning style characteristic of that discipline. That is, the arrows for those departments falling in the accommodative quadrent should point toward the concrete and active extremes of the LSI grid, the arrows for divergent departments toward the concrete and reflective, the arrows for the assimilative departments toward the abstract and reflective and the arrows for the convergent departments toward abstract and active extremes of the LSI grid. The actual results are not so clear-cut. Chemical engineering, mechanical engineering, management, humanities, mathematics and economics all show in varying degrees the predicted accentuation pattern. Potential graduate students in chemistry, civil engineering and electrical engineering score in the convergent quadrent rather than becoming more accommodative. Architecture, biology and earth science potential graduate students move toward the convergent rather than becoming more divergent. Physics moves into the assimilative quadrent.

The above results should be viewed as only suggestive since several measurement problems prevented a more accurate test of the accentuation hypothesis.[5] To deal with these problems in the measurement of the accentuation process we selected four departments for more intensive case study. Several criteria were used to choose four departments whose learning style demands matched the four dominant learning styles. The four departments chosen and their learning style demand were Mechanical engineering = Accommodator, Humanities = Diverger, Mathematics = Assimilator and Economics = Converger.

To study the career choices of the students in the four departments each student's LSI scores were used to position him on the LSI grid with a notation of the career field he had chosen to pursue after graduation. If the student was planning to attend graduate school his career field was circled. If the accentuation process were operating in the career choices of the students we should find that

those students fall in the same quadrent as the norms of their academic major should be more likely to pursue careers and graduate training directly related to that major while students with learning styles that differ from their discipline norms should be more inclined to pursue other careers and not attend graduate school in their discipline. We can illustrate this pattern by examining students in the mathematics department (Figure 5). Ten of the 13 mathematics students (80%) whose learning styles are congruent with departmental norms choose careers and graduate training in mathematics. Only two of the 13 students (15%) whose learning styles are not congruent plan both careers and graduate training in math (these differences are significant using the Fisher Exact Test $p<.01$). Similar patterns occured in the other three departments.

To further test the accentuation process in the four departments we examined whether the student's choice/experience career development cycle indeed operated as an accentuating positive feedback loop. If this were so then those students whose learning style dispositions matched and were reinforced by their discipline demands should show a greater commitment to their choice of future career field than those whose learning styles were not reinforced by their experiences in their discipline. As part of a questionniare students were asked to rate how important it was for them to pursue their chosen career field. In all four departments the average importance rating was higher for the students with a match between learning style and discipline norms (the differences being statistically significant in the mechanical engineering and economics departments). Thus it seems that learning experiences that reinforce learning style dispositions tend to produce greater commitment in career choices than those learning experiences that do not reinforce learning style dispositions.

Summary and Conclusions - Theoretical Considerations

From the above research we draw two main conclusions. First the experiential learning typology seems to provide a useful grid for mapping individual differences in learning style and for mapping corresponding differences in the environmental demands of different career paths. As such it is a potentially powerful tool for describing the differentiated paths of adult development. Secondly, the above data present enticing if not definitive evidence that early career choices tend to follow a path toward accentuation of one's learning style. Learning experiences congruent with learning styles tend to positively influence the choice of future learning and work experiences that reinforce that particular learning style. On the other hand, those students who find a learning environment

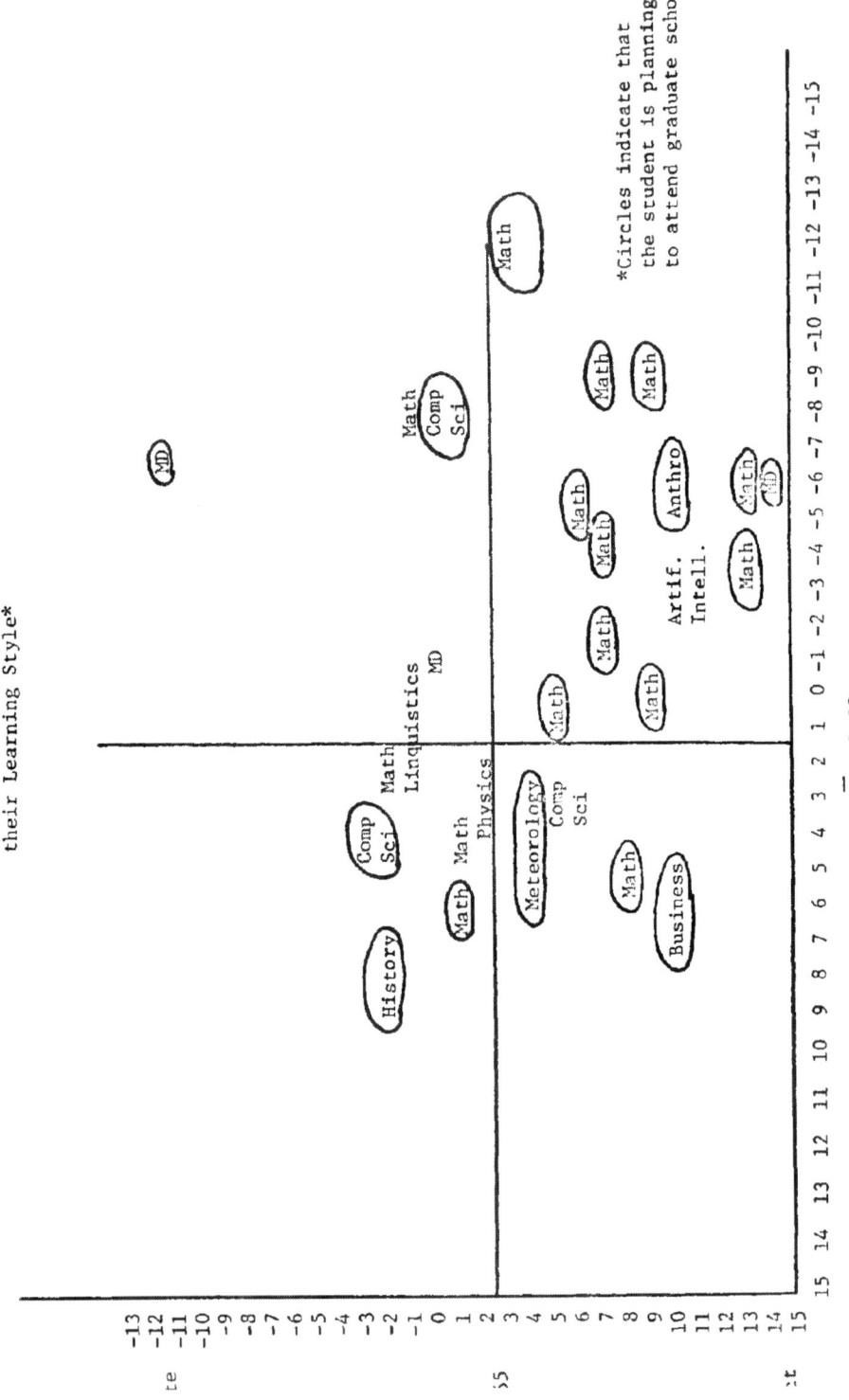

Figure 5. Career field and graduate school plans for Mathematics majors as a function of their Learning Style*

*Circles indicate that the student is planning to attend graduate school.

in future learning and work choices. The research to date suggests that accentuation is the most powerful force in early career development Correspondingly, the major cause of change or deviation from accentuation in early career results from the first reason for change that we identified at the beginning of the research review, i.e. individual choice errors in choosing a career environment that matchs the individual style The primary reason for the strength of the accentuation forces in early career seems to stem from identity pressures to choose a job and a career Fulfillment needs seem to be second priority at this time

We expect however, that this pattern changes in mid-career Specifically we expect that as individuals mature accentuation forces play a smaller role. Changes in career will result more from the second and third reasons we described earlier, namely withdrawl of reward for accentuation and emerging needs for personal fulfillment. Fulfillment needs will take the form of a desire to express non-dominant learning styles, (e.g. concrete and reflective skills for convergent engineers). The origins of these needs stem both from intrapersonal developmental processes (e.g maturation) and external pressures for better managing life tasks (e.g. a man has so emphasized his convergent skills at work that he has neglected home and family)

For many individuals however, withdrawl of reward for accentuation may be a precondition for the emergence of fulfillment concerns Our notion here is that rewards for accentuation are often so powerful and overwhelming that the individual developes what we call a role-encapsulated ego. That is, rewards for specialized role performance tend to prevent the emergence of non-dominant fulfillment needs. Thus, in many cases withdrawl of these rewards may have to precede the awareness of fulfillment needs

The directions of career transition can be predicted from the experiential learning theory of adult development. Since this theory suggests that the process of career change is a learning process that requires not only the acquisition of new skills but also the development of a modified learning style; career transitions to adjacent learning styles (e.g from converger to accommodator or assimilator) should be easier than transitions to opposite learning styles (e.g. from diverger to converger). In addition our clinical observations, although few in number, suggest that it is easier to move from abstract to concrete and from reflective to active than the reverse

Practical Considerations

A better understanding of career transition processes in mid-career can be of great practical importance. As the rates of social and technological change continue to increase in American society the relationships between education and work will of necessity be dramatically altered. At present however, social responses to these changes have lagged far behind. The public and private educational system remains structured to respond to traditional stable notions of career development that are no longer appropriate. Although today the career paths of many men and women may pass through two, three of four distinct phases, each of which require major new learning of knowledge skills and attitudes, educational programs remain primarily oriented to the early stages of life. In most educational institutions adult and continuing education are low status, low priority activities done half-heartedly in the name of community service. The provision of mid-career educational programs has been left primarily to private industry. While this is in some cases as it should be and some of these programs are of quite high quality, all too often the implicit price for admission is a further commitment to one's previous career path. Changing careers is somewhat harder. For example, selection criteria for mid-career programs often include previous experience in that career, and tax laws allow deductions for training that is job related, but not for changing jobs.

In addition to the need for educational programs designed to provide new knowledge and skills for people in career transition, there is a great need for improved, more widely accessible counseling services for these people. The mid-career transition process can be quite traumatic. It is often accompanied by drastic changes in life style and self-concept. Initiating a career transition and working it through successfully can be greatly facilitated by counseling programs designed with an understanding of the developmental dynamics of the career transition process.

The failure to provide avenues for career change produces great losses both in social productivity and in human satisfaction. Organizations do not benefit by locking their employees into careers that long ago ceased to be rewarding and challenging. Society loses the creativity and productivity of those who are barred from entry into new careers in mid-life. This is particularly true of the resources of the female half of the population. Traditional adult developmental patterns for women have included a phase where marriage and family keep them from the job market in their early career. Though social norms are changing, entry into careers in mid-life when family demands are less pressing

still remains difficult for women.

    The theoretical and practical considerations discussed point to the importance of further study of career development, particularly the mid-career transition process from the perspective of an adult developmental model. Experiential learning theory provides one such model that has yielded some interesting results and prospects. It is the intention of this discussion that others in the field be stimulated to explore the issues of adult development and mid-career transition further.

Footnotes

1. The details of the inventory construction along with preliminary reliability and validity studies are described in Kolb (1971). The inventory itself along with management norms appears in Kolb, Rubin and McIntyre, <u>Organizational Psychology: An Experiential Approach</u>, Prentice-Hall, 1971

2. The reason that there are 4 dominant styles is that AC and CE are highly negatively correlated as are RO and AE. Thus individuals who score high on both AC and CE or on both AE and CE with less frequency than do the other four combinations of LSI scores

3. Many of these differences in LSI scores among disciplines are highly statistically significant expecially when they are grouped into physical sciences, social sciences, and the arts (see Kolb, 1971 for details)

Some cautions are in order in interpreting this data. First, is should be remembered that all of the individuals in the sample are managers or managers-to-be. In addition most of these people have completed or are in graduate school. These two facts should produce learning styles that are somewhat more active and abstract than the population at large (As indicated by total sample mean scores on AC-CE and AE-RO cf +4.5 and +2.9 respectively) The interaction between career, high level of education and undergraduate major may produce distinctive learning styles. For example, physicists who are not in industry may be somewhat more reflective than those in this sample. Secondly, undergraduate majors are described only in the most gross terms. There are many forms of engineering or psychology. A business major at one school can be quite different than that at another

4. "t" tests for significance of difference between groups on the abstract/concrete dimension yield the following 1-tail probabilities that are less than .10. Marketing is more concrete that personnel ($p < .10$), engineering ($p < .05$), research ($p < .005$) and finance ($p < .005$) Finance and research are more abstract than personnel (on both comparisons $p < .005$). On the active/reflective dimension research is more reflective than marketing ($p < .05$), engineering ($p < .05$), and to a lesser extent finance ($p < .10$).

5. The first problem was that it was difficult to determine whether a student was in all cases planning graduate training in the subject he majored in. It was difficult, for example, to determine whether a mathematics student planning graduate work in artificial intelligence would continue studying mathematics or not. While most students clearly planned graduate training in the field of their major, the few borderline cases do contaminate the results. A second measurement problem lies in the fact, already demonstrated, that graduate study in general for MIT students is associated with an abstract and active orientation. Since all six of the departments that did not follow the accentuation prediction showed a tendency toward abstractness and four of the six showed a tendency toward the active orientation, this general tendency for graduate study may well have overshadowed the accentuation process in those departments. The final measurement problem has to do with the prediction of learning demands for those departments like electrical engineering who score close to the middle of the LSI grid.

References

1. Bruner, Jerome A., *Essays for the Left Hand*, New York, Antheneum, 1966.

2. Bruner, Jerome A., The Process of Education, New York: Vintage Books, 1960.

3. Bruner, J.S., Goodnow, J.J. and Austin, G.A. *A Study of Thinking*, New York: Wiley and Sons, 1956.

4. Davis, J.A. *Undergraduate Career Decisions*, Aldine Publishing Company, 1965.

5. Erickson, Eric, Indetity and the Life Cycle, *Psychological Issues*, 1959, 1, no. 1.

6. Feldman, Kenneth and Newcomb, Theodore, *The Impact of College on Students*, Jassey-Bass, 1969, Vols. 1 and II.

7. Flavell, John, *The Developmental Psychology of Jean Piaget*, New York: Van Nostrand Reinhold Co., 1963.

8. Gardner, et al. Cognitive Controls, *Psychological Issues*, Vol. 1, no. 4, 1969.

9. Goldstein, K. and Scheerer, M., Abstract and concrete behavior: An experimental study with special tests, *Psychological Monographs*, 1941, 53, no. 239.

10. Growchow, Jerrold, Cognitive Style as a factor in the design of interactive decision-support systems, Ph.D. Thesis, M.I.T. Sloan School, 1973.

11. Harvey, O.J., David Hunt and Harold Schroder, *Conceptual Systems and Personality Organization*, New York: John Wiley, 1961.

12. Holland, J.L. *Making Vocational Choices: A Theory of Careers*, Englewood Cliffs, N.J., 1973.

13. Hudson, Liam, *Contrary Imaginations*, Middlesex, England: Penguin Books Ltd., 1966.

14. Hunt, D.E., *Matching Models in Education: The Coordination of Teaching Methods with Student Characteristics*, Toronto: Ontario Institute for Studies in Education, 1971.

15. Jung, C.G., *Psychological Types*, London: Pantheon Books, 1923.

16. Kagan, Jerome, Bernice L. Rosman, Deborah Day, Joseph Alpert, and William Phillips, Information processing in the child: Significance of Analytic and Reflective Attitudes. *Psychological Monographs*, 78, No. 1, 1964.

17. Kolb, David A. Individual Learning Styles and the Learning Process, M.I.T. Sloan School Working Paper no. 535-71, 1971.

18. Kolb, David, Irwin Rubin and James McIntyre, Organizational Psychology An Experiential Approach, Englewood Cliffs, N.J. Prentice-Hall, Inc., 1971.

19. Kolb, David, Irwin Rubin and Edgar Schein, The MIT Freshmen Integration Research Project A Summary Report, unpulblished report, MIT, 1972.

20. Kolb, David A., On Management and the Learning Process, M.I.T. Sloan School Working Paper No 652-73, March 1973

21. Kolb, David A., Toward a Typology of Learning Styles and Learning Environments. An Investigation of the Impact of Learning Styles and Discipline Demands on the Academic Performance, Social Adaptation and Career Choices of M I T Seniors, M I T Sloan School Working Paper No. 688-73, December 1973b.

22. McClelland, D C On the psychodynamics of creative physical scientists in Contemporary Approaches to Creative Thinking, (ed.) Gruber, H.E. et al. New York Atherton, 1962

23. McCloskey, H and J.H Schaar, Psychological dimensions of anomie, American Psychological Review, 1963, 30, (1) pp 14-40

24. Olsen, M. in Robinson J P and Shauer, P R Measures of Social Psychological Attitudes, Institute for Social Research, University of Michigan, August, 1969, pp. 181-183

25. Plovnick, Mark S. "A Cognitive Theory of Occupational Role", MIT Sloan School of Management Working Paper, No. 524-71, April, 1971.

26. Plovnick, Mark S. "Social Awareness and Role Innovation in Engineers," M.I.T. Sloan School Working Paper, 1972

27. Plovnick, Mark S., "Individual Learning Styles and the Process of Career Choice in Medical Students" Doctoral Thesis in progress, Sloan School of Management, MIT, April, 1974

28. Roe, Anne, The Psychology of Occupations, New York Wiley, 1956

29. Rubin, Irwin, Managing the Learning Process, Sloan School Working Paper, no. 460-70, Sept. 1970

30. Schwitzgebel, Ralph and Kolb, David A., Changing Human Behavior Principles of Planned Intervention, New York McGraw-Hill, 1974

31. Sheehy, Gail, Catch 30 and other predictable crises of growing up adult, New York, Feb, 1974, pp. 30-44

32. Singer, Jerome, The importance of Daydreaming, Psychology Today, 1968, 1, No. 11, pp 18-26

33. Sofer, Cyril, Man in Mid-Career, Cambridge Cambridge University Press, 1970.

34. Stabell, Charles, The Impact of a Conversational Computer System on Human Problem Solving Behavior, unpublished working paper, M I T. Sloan School, 1973.

35. Strasmore, Martin, The Strategic Function Re-evaluated from the Organization Development Perspective, M.I.T. Sloan School Master's Thesis, June 1973

36. Torrealba, David, Convergent and Divergent Learning Styles, MS thesis, M I T Sloan School, 1972.

37. Tough, Allen, The Adult's Learning Projects, Toronto, Ontario Ontario Institute for Studies in Education, 1971

38. Witkin, H.A., Lewis, H.B., Hertzman, M., Machover, K., Meissner, P B., and Wagner, S., Personality Through Perception, New York: Wiley, 1956.

Lightning Source UK Ltd.
Milton Keynes UK
UKHW050724080620
364642UK00004B/315